OLYSLAGER AUTO LIBRARY

British Cars of the Early Fifties 1950-1954

compiled by the OLYSLAGER ORGANISATION
research by David J. Voller
edited by Bart H. Vanderveen

FREDERICK WARNE & Co Ltd
London and New York

THE OLYSLAGER AUTO LIBRARY

This book is one of a growing range of titles on major transport subjects
Titles published so far include:

The Jeep
Cross-Country Cars from 1945
Half-Tracks
Scammell Vehicles
Tanks and Transport Vehicles of World War 2
Fire-Fighting Vehicles 1840–1950
Earthmoving Vehicles
Wreckers and Recovery Vehicles
Passenger Vehicles 1893–1940
Buses and Coaches from 1940
Fairground and Circus Transport

American Cars of the 1930s
American Cars of the 1940s
American Cars of the 1950s
American Trucks of the Early Thirties
American Trucks of the Late Thirties

British Cars of the Early Thirties
British Cars of the Late Thirties
British Cars of the Early Forties
British Cars of the Late Forties
British Cars of the Early Fifties
British Cars of the Late Fifties

Library of Congress Catalog Card No. 74-21047

ISBN 0 7232 1822 6

Filmset and printed in Great Britain
by BAS Printers Limited, Wallop, Hampshire
282.774

INTRODUCTION

The early fifties was a critical time for the British motor industry—as it was, of course, for all industry. The affects of the Second World War were still very much in evidence and the rebuilding process looked like being a long, hard slog.

The motor industry's brief from the Government was clear: to produce as many vehicles as was humanly possible, with the limited raw materials and resources, and then to export them by the shipload. The results were fantastic! Bearing in mind that before the war British annual car exports were always way below the 100,000 mark the industry achieved something of a miracle in becoming the envy overseas of industries that had been exporting in a big way for very many years. In 1951, for example, Britain exported just over 368,000 cars compared with about 217,000 American cars from the United States whose industry was the acknowledged leader in automobile production!

All this activity abroad meant, alas, that the poor old British motorist was merely a spectator who could not get his hands on a new car for love nor money—nor on a second-hand one, for prices were at a prohibitive level for most people. At the start of the decade it was estimated that of the 2 million car owners in the country, over 80% were driving around in pre-war models. Happily the situation was to improve so that by the mid-fifties—with the export drive having levelled out and raw materials becoming more plentiful—a new car for the average home car buyer was no longer a pipe dream.

It was during this early part of the fifties that car manufacturers were really able to shake off the shackles of turning out face-lifted versions of pre-war designs and get down to producing something new. As it transpired, many of the models introduced during that period have been written and talked about on countless occasions over the years and, no doubt, will be for many years to come—cars such as the Bentley Continental, the Triumph TR2, the D-type Jaguar, the Austin A30, the Rover P4 and the Austin-Healey 100, to name but a few.

This book, which follows the same pattern as previous Olyslager Auto Library titles covering British cars of 1930 to 1949, illustrates and briefly describes a broad cross-section of the many models produced from 1950 until 1954. The second half of this fascinating period of development is covered in a separate volume entitled *British Cars of the Late Fifties.*

Piet Olyslager MSIA MSAE KIVI

1950

The British public flocked to the 1949 Earls Court Motor Show to look at the 1950 models which they had little chance of owning for many, many months—if at all—even if they could afford to buy. There was little respite either for those motorists who turned to the second-hand car market because the prices of year-old used cars were, generally speaking, well above list price. The monthly production average during 1950 was 43,543 of which 25,749 (complete) and 4,968 (chassis only) were for export. Total car production for the year was 522,515 and 397,688 of these were exported. New UK registrations totalled 134,394 cars and 11,486 hackneys. Only 1375 cars were imported, valued at £359,005. The value of cars exported was more than £116¼ million. Design trends were favouring full-width bodies, enclosed rear wheels and smaller wheels with a larger tyre section. In an effort to create more room inside, many car designers were opting for three-seater front bench seats which meant that the position of the gear lever had to be moved from the floor to the steering column. Notable newcomers introduced during the year included the Aston Martin DB2, Jowett Jupiter, MG Midget TD, Rover 75 and Triumph Mayflower.

4B Allard J2

4C Allard J2

4B/C: Allard J2 Sports Roadster. The specimens shown were powered by a 6-litre engine and a 440 CID Chrysler V8 respectively (to customer's requirements)—more usual were modified Ford V8 power units. The J2 was superseded by the modified J2X in the autumn of 1951. A two-door Saloon (Model P1) was also available.

4A AC 2-Litre

4A: AC 2-Litre Buckland Sports Tourer. This model had all-new open coachwork by Buckland Body Works of Buntingford, Herts, and was distinguishable from the earlier 2-Litre Drophead Coupé mainly by the full-length front wings and the one-piece, fold-flat windscreen. It was made until 1954.

4D: Alvis Three Litre, Model TA 21 Saloon had a similar body to the Fourteen (discontinued in October 1950), but was larger and followed more the classical line, with sweepingly curved wings, faired-in headlamps and traditional grille.

4D Alvis Three Litre

5A Armstrong Siddeley Typhoon, Lancaster, Hurricane

5A: Armstrong Siddeley Typhoon Saloon, Lancaster Saloon and Hurricane Drophead Coupé. Powered by a 2·3-litre 18 HP engine which developed 75 bhp at 4200 rpm, with a choice of either preselector or synchromesh gearboxes. All three models were introduced in September 1949 to replace the previous 16 HP 1·9-litre-engined versions. The Typhoon was discontinued in May 1950.

5B: Armstrong Siddeley Whitley Saloon was introduced in September 1949. Dimensionally similar to the Lancaster, but with semi razor-edged body styling and greater rear seat headroom, it used the same mechanical components as the Lancaster, Hurricane and Typhoon. Wheelbase of all models was 9 ft 7 in.

5C: Aston Martin DB2 Saloon, first officially shown to the public at the New York Motor Show in April 1950, although a prototype version was entered—successfully—in competitions the previous year. The 2·6-litre twin-OHC engine, which produced 105 bhp at 5000 rpm, was fitted in an all-new light-alloy body; the bonnet and wing structure was hinged at the front so that with the bonnet raised the entire front end of the chassis could be exposed.

5C Aston Martin DB2

5D: Austin A40 Models GS2 Devon Saloon (shown) and GP2 Countryman were carryovers from 1949 with detail modifications. The Devon was also available with bench-type front seat; this version was designated Devon Mark II, Model GS2A.

5D Austin A40

5B Armstrong Siddeley Whitley

1950

6A Austin A70

6A: **Austin** A70
Models BS2 Hampshire
Saloon (shown) and BW3
Countryman for 1950 had
triangular vent panels in the front
windows, like the 1950 A40
models (*see* 5D).

6B: **Austin** A90 Atlantic Sports saloon, Model BE2,
was introduced in September 1949. Powered by a
2·6-litre 88-bhp engine it was mechanically
similar to the A90 Atlantic Convertible but with a
higher axle ratio. Distinctive body styling featured
front wings that swept through to the rear of the
body, a wrap-round rear window and a cyclops
type built-in spotlamp.

6C: **Austin** A125 Sheerline Model DS1 luxury saloon had a
six-cylinder 3·9-litre engine. Model DM1 Limousine was similar
but had a lengthened chassis, different seating and other detail differences.

6D Bristol 401

6D: **Bristol** 401 Saloon had a 2-litre 85-bhp
Six engine and a top speed of 100 mph. The
body was built by Bristol under Superleggera
Touring patents and included concealed locks
for fuel filler and luggage compartment. The
bumpers had synthetic rubber inserts.

6E: **Citroën** Light Fifteen
was the British-built edition
of the French Citroën 11
Sport. It featured a walnut
fascia board and other
distinguishing differences,
including wheels, bumpers,
chromium-plated radiator
grille, etc. Production ran
from 1945 until 1955.

6B Austin A90

6C Austin A125

6E Citroën Light Fifteen

7A Daimler Straight Eight

7A: **Daimler** Straight Eight DE36 chassis with Sports Saloon bodywork by Freestone and Webb. Other luxury cars were built on this chassis by well-known firms such as Hooper, Windover, etc.

7B: **Daimler** DB18 Consort saloon differed from the earlier version (2½-litre DB18) by having a curved radiator grille, faired-in headlamps and sidelamps, and curved V-section bumpers. Mechanical improvements included a hypoid bevel final drive and hydro-mechanical brakes.

7C Dellow Mark I

7C: **Dellow** Mark I Sports started life as a one-off trials special—the creation of K. C. Delingpole and R. B. Lowe (hence Dellow). In October 1949 it was introduced as a small-series production car, featuring a Ford Ten E93A engine (a supercharger was optional) and gearbox with Ford rigid front and rear axles, steering and brakes. The body was aluminium.

7D: **Ford** Prefect Model E493A was continued from 1949 with no changes. It had been given a restyled front end early in that year and had an 1172-cc 30-bhp L-head Four engine with three-speed gearbox.

7E: **Ford** Pilot Model E71A Saloon was also a carryover from the previous year. It was powered by a 3·6-litre V8 engine. Production ceased in 1951. The two-door Anglia (E494A) was also continued unchanged (*see* 17A).

7B Daimler DB18 Consort

7D Ford Prefect

7E Ford Pilot

8A Ford Pilot

8C Healey Silverstone

8A: **Ford** Pilot V8 Estate Car with all-metal panelled body by Hawes & Son Ltd was introduced in 1950 and produced only in small numbers. This surviving specimen was registered a few years later. The spare wheel was mounted on the tailgate.

8B: **Frazer-Nash** Cabriolet was introduced in September 1949. Powered by the Bristol 1971-cc engine—used in similar form on the competition Frazer-Nashes—this luxury tourer had a greater wheelbase and track than the competition models but, nevertheless, had a very low overall height. It featured an ingenious windscreen, which folded down onto the scuttle, and two-folding emergency seats inside. A Mille Miglia two-seater version was also introduced.

8C: **Healey** Silverstone was introduced in July 1949. The open two-seater had a lightweight stressed-skin alloy sports body mounted on a

D-type chassis (E-type chassis from April 1950) and was powered by a 2·5-litre Riley engine. The windscreen was retracted into the scuttle when in the racing position, instead of being folded flat; the spare wheel 'doubled' as a rear bumper and the wings were removable for competition work. Only 105 were built.

8D: **Hillman** Minx Mark IV Saloon, Convertible Coupé (shown) and Estate Car were introduced in December 1949. Although retaining the styling of the Mark III versions they featured more powerful engines (1265 cc *v.* 1184·5 cc) and could be quickly identified by the separate sidelamps. The left-hand drive car shown was owned by an American reporter who is photographed alongside it with a friend, in London, prior to setting off on a tour of Europe.

8B Frazer-Nash Cabriolet

8D Hillman Minx

9A Humber Super Snipe

9A: **Humber** Super Snipe Mark II Saloon. Fitted with the 4086-cc, 100-bhp engine (also used with the Mark I Super Snipes) and a four-speed gearbox, this six-seater model (first introduced in October 1948) incorporated detail changes for 1950 (announced in August 1949) including separate sidelamps below the headlamps. A Humber Imperial Mark II Saloon was launched late in 1949 and was virtually identical to the Pullman Limousine of that time but without the central partition.

9B: **Jaguar** Mark V Drophead Coupé and its Saloon counterpart, were available with a choice of engine—2½-litre or 3½-litre. The Drophead Coupé featured external plated hood-irons. The Mark V models were discontinued in 1951.

9C: **Jowett** Javelin Jupiter Mark I, Series SA, introduced in March 1950, had originated as ERA/Javelin chassis in September 1949. Powered by a flat-4, 1486-cc engine which gave over 60 bhp, this open sports model featured an aluminium panelled body with sweepingly curved wings and a rear luggage boot which could only be reached from inside the car. The whole front of the bodywork was hinged at the scuttle.

9B Jaguar Mark V

9C Jowett Javelin Jupiter

10A Lanchester Ten

10C MG Midget TD

10B Lea-Francis 2½-Litre Sports

10A: **Lanchester** Ten, Series LD10 Saloon. In September 1949 the popular 10 HP chassis was fitted with a new four-light Barker coachbuilt body (aluminium panels on a wood and steel framework) which, although similar in appearance to the previous Briggs (steel) bodied version at the front, had a more attractive line and featured curved windows and a spacious luggage compartment.

10B: **Lea-Francis** 2½-Litre Sports was introduced in September 1949 with similar general lines to the Fourteen Sports which it replaced. It was powered by a twin-carburettor 100-bhp engine and featured doors with wind-up windows and a windscreen with triangular side panels which could be removed as one assembly. It was continued in production until October 1954, when the company folded.

10C: **MG** Midget TD replaced the TC in January 1950. Although powered by the same engine it featured numerous detail improvements, including independent front suspension, rack and pinion steering, and revised gear ratios to suit its greater overall weight. The general outline of the body at the front end was modified on the lines of the Y Series open-tourer (1948–51). Its reception by MG enthusiasts of the day was decidedly cool, mainly because of its 'heavier' look, the pierced disc wheels and, above all, the inclusion of bumpers!

11A Renault 4CV

11B Riley 2½-Litre

11C Rolls-Royce Silver Wraith

11D Rover 75

11A: **Renault** 4CV, Model R1060, was introduced in Britain in November 1949 and assembled at the Renault Ltd plant at Acton, near London; it had originally been introduced in France in 1947. and featured a rear-mounted engine. The cubic capacity of 760 cc meant that it was just over the international 750-cc class for competition events. This was rectified in 1950 when the cylinder bore size was reduced to give it a capacity of 748 cc (R1062).
11B: **Riley** 2½-Litre Model RMC Roadster was produced during 1948–50, but was only available on the home market from September 1949. Originally a three-seater, it became a two-seater early in 1950.

11C: **Rolls-Royce** Silver Wraith Sports saloon, with coachwork by Park Ward & Co, Ltd. One of these models—owned by Mr W. M. Couper—took part in the 1950 Monte Carlo Rally where it won the *Grand Prix d'Honneur du Concours de Confort.*
11D: **Rover 75** Series P4 Saloon was introduced in September 1949, replacing the Series P3. It had completely restyled bodywork, mounted on a new full-length chassis with improved (six-cylinder twin-carb) engine, transmission and suspension. The traditional Rover appearance gave way to full-width styling with an extended boot to balance the front end. A cyclops type foglamp was mounted in the radiator grille.

12A Standard Vanguard

12A: **Standard** Vanguard 20S Saloon and Estate Car for 1950 were modified in various respects, including separate side lights, enclosed rear wheels and relocation of the gearshift lever to the left of the steering column.

12B: **Triumph** Mayflower Saloon, Series 1200T, introduced in September 1949. This two-door, razor-edged, small car had 38-bhp 1247-cc side-valve engine mounted in an integral body/chassis structure with coil-spring IFS. Although the bodywork was basically a scaled-down version of the Renown (q.v.), it was surprisingly roomy inside and had the same internal width (53 in). In October 1950 a limited-production Drophead Coupé version was announced.

12C: **Triumph** Renown Series 20ST Saloon. Renamed version of an earlier model, namely the 2000 Saloon (Series 20T) which, in turn, had been introduced in February 1949 to supersede the 1800 Saloon (Series 18T). Powered by the 2088-cc Standard Vanguard engine, this razor-edged saloon had a box-section type chassis which replaced the tubular type used on the 1800—with independent front suspension and Lockheed hydraulic brakes.

12B Triumph Mayflower

12C Triumph Renown

13A: **Triumph** Roadster (prototype). This ambitious and very advanced model, revealed by Triumph in 1950, was a Vanguard-engined sports car fitted with striking, aerodynamic bodywork and featuring fully retractable electrically-operated headlamp covers, curved windscreen, hydraulically-operated top, windows and seats, large boot with wind-down tray for the spare wheel and a transmission with three speeds and overdrive fourth gear as standard. Triumph decided, alas, that it was too complicated and expensive to produce and could not, therefore, be sold at a competitive price. Only two prototypes were built. (*See* also pages 46, 62 and 63.)

13B: **Vauxhall** Wyvern, Series LIX, was a smaller engined (1442-cc 4-cyl.) stable mate of the Velox saloon (Series LIP). Externally it was similar to the Velox except that the wheels were painted in the body colour (*v*. cream), no bumper overriders were fitted and the tyre size was 5·00-16 (*v*. 5·90-16). Compared with 1949, 1950 editions had larger headlamps with separate sidelamps, plus various mechanical modifications.

13C: **Wolseley** Six-Eighty was a larger companion model to the similarly-styled four-cylinder engined Four-Fifty saloon and powered by a six-cylinder 2215-cc, 72-bhp twin-carburettor engine. It also had a 9 ft 2 in (*v*. 8 ft 6 in) wheelbase and a greater overall length. The separate sidelights were fitted from September. The Six-Eighty was continued until October 1954 when it was replaced by the Six-Ninety.

13B Vauxhall Wyvern

13A Triumph Roadster (prototype)

13C Wolseley Six-Eighty

1951

1951 The need to export and to rearm again left the British public merely dreaming of shiny new cars they had virtually no hope of owning. The monthly British car production average was 39,660 of which 25,749 (complete) and 4968 (chassis only) were exported. British vehicle manufacturers had begun to profit by the abolition of taxation based on the horsepower formula. Unfortunately, much of the benefit derived from the change in the method of taxation was later cancelled out by a further increase in fuel tax.

The President of the SMMT confirmed that Britain's Motor Industry had retained its lead over all other manufacturing industries as the nation's greatest exporter. British car design, generally, reflected a radical change in attitudes towards production processes and manufacturing methods since the war.

Intensive competition in the world's export markets resulted in a greater variety of body styles. Following the uncertainty regarding rearmament demands, the amount of chromium plating on cars started to increase and less sombre colour schemes were in evidence. Although pressed steel was still the popular material for producing body panels, development work was well under way with non-metallic materials such as resin bonded glass-fibre. Despite the use of new materials for interior trim, such as nylon, by manufacturers abroad, the British motor industry remained faithful to leather for many of its cars. A total of 475,919 cars was produced in the UK this year. Exports totalled 368,101, imports 3723. New vehicle registrations amounted to 138,373 cars and 7881 hackneys.

14B Alvis Three Litre

14A: Allard K2 Sports Two-seater, introduced in 1950, replaced the 1946–50 Model K1. Although mechanically similar to its predecessor—including Ford V8 3·6-litre 95-bhp engine, three-speed gearbox, 8 ft 10 in wheelbase—it had various modifications such as coil spring front suspension, a proper luggage boot and a shallower radiator grille, and was more fully equipped. A two-door Saloon (P1) and two-seater Sports Roadster (J2) were also available.

14B: Alvis Three Litre Drophead Coupé was a two-door Tickford-bodied companion to the Saloon (*see* 1950). Featuring similar styling, this attractive coupé had a top that could be either folded flat down or positioned so that only the peak furled, in *coupé-de-ville* fashion. A Sports model (TB 21) was also available. It had similar lines to the model it replaced—the much maligned 1·9-litre (TB 14) Sports—but with one all-important difference: the frontal appearance became typically Alvis again (classic radiator, traditional headlamp position, etc.).

14C: Armstrong Siddeley Eighteen chassis with custom-built Shooting Brake/Utility coachwork by the well-known firm of Bonallack & Sons. From September 1950 until April 1951 Armstrong Siddeley offered a Limousine model on a special long-wheelbase (10 ft 2 in) chassis.

14A Allard K2

14C Armstrong Siddeley Eighteen

15A Aston Martin DB2

15C Austin A70

15B Austin A40

15D Austin A70

15A : **Aston Martin** DB2 Convertible was introduced in October 1950. Mechanically similar to the DB2 Saloon (*see* 1950), this version was fitted with wind-up windows and a top that stowed away neatly without spoiling the generally smooth lines of the body. A special high-performance 120-bhp Vantage engine became optionally available for both models.

15B : **Austin** A40 range comprised the Devon Saloon (GS2), Sports (GD2, *see* following page) and Countryman (GP3, illustrated) as well as Van and Pickup models. From August 1951 the GS2 and GP3 had a new fascia, and other modifications, and became GS3 and GP4 respectively.

15C : **Austin** A70 Hereford, Model BS3, Saloon. Although this model used the same chassis as the earlier A70 Hampshire (Model BS2), its body was larger, roomier and more rounded. It was more popular than its predecessor and had a production run of four years. A Drophead Coupé version was also available ; the top was operated manually on this model, although power operation was available at extra cost.

15D : **Austin** A70 Hereford Countryman (Model BW4) was the Estate Car version, featuring a wood-framed body with metal roof. A Pickup version (BK3) was also available. The A70 Hereford range continued in production, with no material changes, until October 1954.

16A: **Austin** A40 Sports, Model GD2. Open four-seater with full-width frontal styling on Continental lines. This model was based, mechanically, on the A40 Saloon model, but with various modifications—including the fitting of twin carburettors on the 1200-cc power unit which gave an output of 46 bhp at 4400 rpm, strengthening the chassis by welding a pressed steel floor to the top and bottom of the main members and adopting full hydraulic operation for the brakes (standard on all A40 models from August 1951). When not in use the top folded away neatly behind the rear seat squab. The alloy bodywork was produced by Jensen.

16B: **Bentley** Mark VI models continued into 1951 without significant changes. The version shown is a two-door Drophead Coupé, custom built by Park Ward. A two-door Clubman Coupé version was also available.

16C: **Bristol** 401 Saloon continued with detail modifications. Among the changes were the introduction of chromium-plated metal strips with small overriders to replace the rubber bumper inserts, the deletion of the side scuttle vents and lower body-edge mouldings and the inclusion of new style headlamps and a polished wood fascia panel. The 401 continued in production until September 1953. (*See* also 38.)

For Town or Country

16B Bentley Mark VI

16A Austin A40 Sports

16C Bristol 401

17A Ford Anglia

17B Ford Consul

17C Ford Zephyr Six

17A: **Ford** Anglia Model E494A was continued in production virtually unchanged from October 1948 until October 1953. For Prefect *see* 7D.

17B: **Ford** Consul Model EOTA Saloon. Powered by a new four-cylinder 1·5-litre overhead-valve engine which developed 47 bhp at 4400 rpm. Dimensionally similar to the new Zephyr Six—Consul bonnet and wheelbase were both slightly shorter—this model was visibly different by its low set horizontal grille with vertical slats. Both the Consul and Zephyr Six were of entirely new integral chassisless construction—like the OHV engines a complete break with Ford tradition. They were introduced in October of 1950 for the 1951 model year.

17C: **Ford** Zephyr Six Model EOTTA Saloon was powered by a new six-cylinder 2·3-litre OHV engine which developed 68 bhp at 4000 rpm. The Zephyr Six and its companion Consul (*q.v.*) caused something of a sensation when they were revealed, as the styling was so different from that of previous Fords. Both cars had full width slab-sided bodies, curved windscreens and four doors.

17D: **Frazer-Nash** Mille Miglia I Sports. Attractive two-seater powered by a triple-carburettor 1971-cc engine and using the standard 8 ft wheelbase. Centrelock, pierced disc wheels were standard. In common with the Cabriolet (*see* 1950), this model had a broader version of the marque's traditional grille with horizontal bars.

17D Frazer-Nash Mille Miglia I

18A Healey Tickford Saloon

18A : **Healey** Tickford Saloon, introduced in October 1950. Powered by the popular 2½-litre Riley engine, this two-door, four-seater sports saloon was based on the earlier Healey Elliot Saloon (1946–50) but with modified styling and more comprehensive fittings. The Abbott Drophead Coupé (*see* 1952)—introduced at the same time—was mechanically identical and dimensionally similar to the Tickford Saloon.

18B : **Hillman** Minx Mark IV Saloon (shown), Convertible Coupé (*see* 1950) and Estate Car continued for 1951 without significant changes. These were the only Hillman cars in production at the time.

18C : **Hillman** Minx production line at the Rootes Group Manufacturing Division at Ryton, Coventry. The finished unitary body-cum-chassis assembly was suspended at a convenient working height so that the engine and working parts could be raised and fitted into position.

18B Hillman Minx

18C Hillman Minx

19A HRG Sports

19B Humber Hawk

19A: **HRG** Sports two-seater, one of the classic sports cars produced by HRG Engineering Co. Ltd, Kingston-by-Pass, Tolworth, Surrey between 1935 and 1956. Available with either an 1100-cc (from 1939) or 1500-cc (from 1935) twin-carburettor engine, the open model (shown) changed relatively little through the years although variations on the familiar body style did appear —just after the war (1500 Aerodynamic), and in 1955 (1½-litre Sports/Roadster). HRGs had a reputation for reliability, and, not surprisingly, numerous competition successes including—in the late 1940s—the Belgian 24-hour race (two years running) and the Alpine Trial.

19B: **Humber** Hawk Mark IV, 4-door saloon, which replaced the Mark III for the 1951 model year, featured an increase in cylinder bore diameter (capacity became 2267 cc v. 1944 cc) plus various other engine improvements, a new high-geared steering arrangement and bigger tyres (6·40-15 v. 5·50-15).

19C: **Humber** Pullman Mark III superseded the 1948–50 Mark II and had a revised suspension system—made smoother by doubling the leaf width of the front transverse spring and halving the number of leaves. Although mainly produced in eight-seater limousine form, a Warwick Estate car bodied version (shown) was also available.

19C Humber Pullman

20A Jaguar Mark VII

20B Jaguar XK120

20C Jaguar XK120C

20A: Jaguar Mark VII Saloon was announced in October 1950 and featured entirely new bodywork with full-width styling, bolder curves and a flowing tail. Although this popular four-door model had a very similar chassis to the Mark IV (discontinued in July 1951) it was very much a 'saloon equivalent' to the XK120. The exciting XK120 engine (twin-carburettor, twin-OHC, 3442-cc, 160-bhp) gave it a top speed of over 100 mph. A sliding roof was standard. Well appointed interior; the instrument panel and cappings were finished in figured walnut. It was priced at £1590.

20B: Jaguar XK120. The sensational 3½-litre-engined open Sports model, which had been announced in October 1948, was joined by a fixed-head coupé version (shown) in March 1951. The all-metal top had a considerable window area, yet only increased the weight of the car by 168 lb. Total enclosure of the passenger compartment made it possible to provide a more luxurious interior than on the Sports version.

20C: Jaguar XK120C. Known as the C-type Jaguar, this was a limited-production version for competition work. The fully tuned 3½-litre engine had a 9·0:1 compression ratio and an output of 210 bhp; an 8·0:1 compression ratio version of 200 bhp was optionally available. The body was fitted to a tubular metal framework instead of the laminated ash frame used on the road car. The model shown won the 1951 Le Mans 24-hour race; the wheel was shared by Peter Whitehead and Peter Walker. The pursuing car is a Nash-Healey (a British Healey with an American Nash 3·8-litre OHV Six engine).

21A Jensen Interceptor

21B Lanchester Fourteen

Exclusive   Design   ——   Impressive   Performance

All models are powered by four-cylinder engines of Lea-Francis design and
manufacture incorporating the patented overhead-valve gear.
The cars are fast and fascinating to handle and the Girling Hydraulic braking
system is powerful, safe and sure.
The 2½-litre Sports has a Two/Four-Seater body that is practical and comfort-
able and the 14 h.p. Four-Light Saloon is a Four/Five-Seater with a luxurious
finish throughout.

LEA - FRANCIS CARS LIMITED, COVENTRY, ENGLAND

21C Lea-Francis

21A: Jensen Interceptor Cabriolet had full-width styling—with seating
for 5–6 people—and was powered by a 3993-cc Austin Six engine which
had an output of 130 bhp. The entire rear panel and quarters of the top
were of Perspex. In 1950 small air-intakes were added either side of the
radiator grille to cool the brakes, and larger tyres were fitted.
21B: Lanchester Fourteen Saloon as announced in October 1950 had
more up-to-date body styling than the Ten (*see* 1950) which was
discontinued in July 1951. Powered by a new 1968-cc engine which
developed 60 bhp at 4200 rpm it sold at £1364. The Leda (introduced in
1952) which was similarly styled and equipped was an all-steel bodied

version for the export market. A De-Ville Convertible was introduced in
1952 (*see* 1953).
21C: Lea-Francis Fourteen four-light Saloon was introduced in October
1950. Powered by the 1767-cc 65-bhp engine with a four-speed gearbox
this four/five-seater was styled on traditional lines, unlike the more modern
sweeping appearance of the Fourteen Mark VI six-light Saloon which
was redesignated the 14/70 (in 1950) until it ceased production in 1951.
The 2½-Litre Sports (background) continued unchanged (*see also* 1950).

22A: **Marauder** Type A Sports Tourer, introduced in August 1950. This very attractive three-seater open model had evolved from ideas developed in a single-seater sprint racing car, by a group of enthusiasts with Rover connections. Understandably the Marauder was based on Rover components which included a shortened Rover 75 chassis, with coil spring IFS, a twin-carburettor, tuned version of Rover 75 2·1-litre engine which had an output of 80 bhp at 4200 rpm and four-speed gearbox with overdrive (unless fitted with freewheel). Certain modifications were made in 1951, at which time a more powerful (Type 100) version became available. Delayed production, changes in the market conditions and increased costs led to the car being priced out of its class by double purchase tax; production ceased in the summer of 1952. Only about 15 cars in all were built.

22B: **Morgan** Plus Four was a larger-engined (Standard Vanguard, 2088-cc, 68 bhp at 4200 rpm) replacement for the long running 4/4 which had been in production, with relatively few changes, since the late 1930s. Available as a two-seater Sports or Drophead Coupé (shown) the Plus Four had numerous other improvements, including a strengthened chassis, slightly longer wheelbase, more accurate front suspension/steering geometry and a somewhat softer ride. A four-seater version was added later in 1951 (*see* 1952).

22C: **Morris** Minor, Series MM, four-door Saloon was announced in October 1950 as an addition to the popular two-door Saloon and Convertible versions which had been introduced in 1948. Apart from the different door arrangement, this version was externally distinguishable from the other two by having larger headlamps set high in the wings, with separate sidelamps positioned alongside the radiator grille. Early in 1951 this modification was also incorporated on the two-door models. Other improvements common to all versions were twin windscreen wipers and one-piece bumpers. A painted radiator grille in place of chromium was introduced in March 1951.

22B Morgan Plus Four

22C Morris Minor

22A Marauder Type A

23A Morris Oxford

23B Paramount Ten

23C Riley 2½-Litre

23D Rover 75

23A : **Morris** Oxford with a difference ! This 1951 car was, later in its life, converted into a tractive unit for a light semi-trailer.

23B : **Paramount** Ten. Although series production did not start until early in 1951, prototype versions were in evidence during 1949/50. Powered by a 1172-cc Ford engine with twin carburettors—a supercharger was optional—and using a Ford three-speed gearbox the attractive Paramount (initially available as a Roadster or Drophead Coupé) had a chequered career during which time it passed through four changes of ownership. A 1½-litre-engined model replaced the Ten a matter of months before production finally ceased in 1956.

23C : **Riley** 2½-Litre Saloon was in production from 1946 to 1953 with only minor detail modifications. During 1948–51 a Drophead Coupé version was available ; a Roadster (*see* 11B) was made during 1948–50. The contemporary 1½-Litre Saloon was similar in appearance, but had slightly shorter wheelbase and dark blue instead of light blue radiator badge.

23D : **Rover** 75 P4 Saloon was carryover from 1950 (*q.v.*) and was the only car produced by The Rover Co. Ltd at the time, except for the Land-Rover multi-purpose vehicle (Series I ; wb 80 in, 86 in from August 1951).

24A Singer Nine

24B Singer Nine

24A/B: **Singer** Nine Model 4AB Roadster, introduced in October 1950, was an improved version of the Model 4A (launched in Sept. 1949). Modifications included a shorter radiator with a small valance at its base, longer and sweeping front wings, fixed bonnet sides and centrally hinged bonnet top, plain bumpers, full disc type wheels, improved seats, larger brakes and independent front suspension with coil springs. The Model AB, which sold at £666, was discontinued in October 1951. Also available were the SM1500 Saloon and Roadster.

24C: **Standard** Vanguard I models (first introduced in 1948; modified versions for 1950 easily distinguishable by full spats over the rear wheels) were continued into 1951 with no modifications of note. Available were a four-door Saloon and Estate Car (shown), both fitted with a four-cylinder, 2088-cc power unit which developed 68 bhp at 4200 rpm. Laycock-de-Normanville overdrive became optionally available in the summer of 1950; the Vanguard was one of the first British cars to offer this facility. Prices were £726 for the Saloon and £877 for the Estate Car.

24C Standard Vanguard

25A Sunbeam-Talbot 90

25C Triumph Mayflower

25B Sunbeam-Talbot 90

25D Vauxhall Velox

25A: **Sunbeam-Talbot** 90 Mark II Saloon was powered by a larger engine than the Mark I (2267 cc v. 1944 cc) which gave it a significantly better performance. Other modifications made to this popular marque were a stiffer chassis frame with coil-spring IFS, anti-sway bar at the front, transverse bar at the rear, hypoid bevel rear axle with higher gearing, and a new heating and ventilation system. The Mark II could be identified by the modified front end which included two small air-intakes next to the radiator grille, the new style bumpers and separate sidelamps.

25B: **Sunbeam-Talbot** 90 Mark II Drophead Coupé, which was approximately 60 lb lighter than the Saloon version, had wind-up windows not only in the doors but also in the rear quarters.

25C: **Triumph** Mayflower Drophead Coupé. Announced in October 1950, only eleven of these were made, the last in the early part of 1951. The Mayflower Saloon (see 1950) continued with a number of modifications including a revised rear suspension and more deeply dished road wheels.

25D: **Vauxhall** Motors Ltd were still using a pre-war bodyshell for their Wyvern and Velox (shown) models, albeit with new front and rear end styling (from 1948) and other modifications. These models were in production until the summer of 1951.

1952

The monthly British car production average during this year was 37,334 of which 22,979 (complete) and 2,840 (chassis only) were exported. Although there was still a shortage of new cars for the domestic market things were looking decidedly brighter. The general state of British roads and the Government's attitude towards the problem came in for a great deal of criticism from many quarters. The chairman of The Berkshire Highways Committee said in his report on the condition of that county's roads . . . 'There is a very small margin between the present condition of the roads and a condition which would be wholly unsatisfactory'.

On the design front overhead-valve engines were rapidly replacing the side-valve variety and engine sizes were gradually increased. More attention was being given to producing wings and grilles which could be removed easily for repair and—following the demands of overseas buyers —to rust-proofing and dust-sealing. Petrol tanks and spare wheels were to be found in some unexpected places, in the search for more luggage space.

Although many of the models were changed only in detail from the previous year, the public did see the arrival of the new Austin A30 Seven and the restyled Vauxhall Wyvern and Velox.

Of the year's total car production of 448,000 no fewer than 308,942 were exported, valued at nearly £111 million. Imports were down to just under 1900 cars and the total of new car registrations in the UK was 196,469 (including 5432 hackneys).

26B Allard M2X

26A AC 2-Litre

26C Armstrong Siddeley Whitley

26A: **AC** 2-Litre two-door Saloon was continued from the previous years and in October was joined by a four-door model (*see* 1953). The Drophead Coupé had been discontinued but the Buckland Tourer (*see* 1950) was still available.

26B: **Allard** M2X Drophead Coupé was introduced in November 1951, and based on the P1 Saloon (introduced 1949) but with an 'A'-shaped radiator grille and floor-mounted gear-change. This model—powered by a Ford V8 3·6-litre engine—was very much in the Allard tradition. A

modified version of the J2 (*see* 1950) called the J2X was also announced for 1952. The 'X' indicated that in the front suspension arrangement the radius arms were ahead of the front axle.

26C: **Armstrong Siddeley** Whitley six-light Saloon joined the four-light version (*see* 1950) in March 1952. This later version had rear quarter lights added to give extra visibility and the rear of the car was rearranged to provide better leg room. The Lancaster Saloon (*see* 1950) was discontinued in March 1952.

27A : **Aston Martin** DB3 Sports Roadster was a limited-production model, sold primarily for competition work and powered by a six-cylinder 2580-cc (2922-cc from late 1952) double-OHV engine driving through a five-speed gearbox coupled to a DeDion type rear axle. A factory-entered DB3 won the Nine-hour Race at Goodwood in 1952 —the model's first major victory.

27B : **Aston Martin** DB2 Saloon. Models from October 1951 were distinguishable by the one-piece radiator and brake duct grille. In 1952 a privately-owned DB2 came third in the Le Mans 3-litre class and seventh overall.

27A Aston Martin DB3

27B Aston Martin DB2

27C Austin A30

27C : **Austin** A30 Model AS3 Saloon started its successful production run in October 1951. Of conventional layout it featured an 803-cc 28-bhp, OHV Four engine, four-speed gearbox, hypoid-bevel final-drive, coil-spring IFS and semi-elliptic leaf-spring rear suspension, and was the first Austin to use the chassisless integral construction format. Although a four-door car—two-door models were introduced later—rear seat entry was difficult and occupation cramped. It sold at £529 and was initially designated Austin Seven.

28A Austin A40

28B Austin A40

28C Austin A70

28A: **Austin** A40 Somerset Model GS4 Saloon was introduced in February 1952. Virtually a scaled-down version of the A70 Hereford (*see* 1951) this model was mechanically similar to the preceding A40 Devon (1948–52), but with various detail improvements including a slight increase in bhp (42 *v.* 40) from the 1200-cc engine. The new body styling was well planned with wider rear doors giving better access to rear seats, more passenger space and better soundproofing.

28B: **Austin** A40 Somerset Model GD5 Drophead Coupé joined the saloon in August 1952. It had similar dimensions to the saloon except that the overall height was slightly less. The top could be used in three positions, i.e. fully raised, 'coupé de ville' or stowed behind the rear seat. The rear quarter windows could be swivelled down into the body sides.

28C: **Austin** A70 Hereford Model BD3 Drophead Coupé looked much like its A40 counterpart (*see* 28B) but was larger. It was discontinued in July.

28D Bentley Mark VI

28D: **Bentley** Mark VI Saloon. The first significant change since its introduction in 1946 came when the cylinder bore size was increased to 92 mm in October 1951 so giving the engine a 4566-cc cubic capacity. The model shown is a Drophead Coupé by Park Ward & Co. Ltd.

29A: **Daimler** Regency Saloon was announced at the London Motor Show in October 1951. It was a 90-bhp 3-litre-engined, luxury four-door model with modern lines but nevertheless traditionally very much a Daimler. It was built primarily as a result of the strong overseas demand for a large capacity car with good ground clearance, plus six-seater accommodation well hidden by graceful body styling. Surprisingly, only a few of these versions were built. A 3½-litre Regency Mark II did, however, go into production late in 1954.

29B: **Daimler** 3-Litre Convertible Coupé, a Barker-bodied, two-door luxury model built on the 2952-cc Regency chassis in 1952. Engine performance was increased by the use of an aluminium cylinder head and a higher compression ratio which pushed its output up to 100 bhp at 4200 rpm. Features of this model included twin fuel tanks—one beneath each rear wing—and power-operated top, windows and luggage boot lid. Only a few were ever built.

29C Dellow Mark III

29A Daimler Regency

29B Daimler 3-Litre

29C: **Dellow** Mark III Sports Tourer, a four-seater model introduced in April 1952. Based on the two-seater (*see* 1950) but with a 1-foot longer wheelbase; the body was 7 in longer and 2 in wider. Full hood (top) and sidescreens were provided and the sidelamps were moved to the wings. The handiness and feel were somewhat reduced on the four-seater—the turning circle, for example went up by almost 4 feet. Sold at £774.

29D: **Ford** Consul Model EOTA Saloon was a carryover from 1951. In September 1952 the dashboard was revised and the instruments centred round the steering column. Shown in the background is Anne Hathaway's Cottage—the home of Shakespeare's wife —in Stratford-on-Avon.

29D Ford Consul.

30A Ford Consul

30C Healey 3-Litre

30B Ford Pilot

30D Healey Abbott D/H Coupé

30A : **Ford** Consul (shown) and Zephyr Six Drophead Coupés were mechanically similar to their respective saloon versions. These two-door models had a folding top which could be power-operated to the halfway position ; manual operation was required to close it fully or to take it back to this position. Unlike the saloons, they had a divided front seat, each section being separately adjustable with a tilting squab.

30B : **Ford** Pilot V8 was officially discontinued the previous year but this surviving export model was supplied in 1952. Fitted with Shooting Brake bodywork it was based on the commercial pickup chassis/cab with 3·89 axle ratio and rod/cable rear brakes.

30C : **Healey** 3-Litre Sports Convertible (Series G) with Alvis engine and gearbox had similar body styling to the earlier Nash-Healey Sports Roadster which was made for and sold on the export market during 1950–52 (a modified version followed up until the end of 1954). Popularly known as the Alvis-Healey, it had a two/three-seater Healey-built body with full weather equipment. The 2993-cc power unit developed 106 bhp at 4200 rpm. Only 25 were built.

30D : **Healey** Abbott Drophead Coupé was a two-door soft-top version of the Tickford Saloon (see 1951). From approximately November 1951 onwards it was built on an F-type chassis. Only 77 were made (1950–54).

31A: **Hillman** Minx Mark V Saloon replaced the Mark IV in October 1951, the only visible differences being chrome side strips along the body, side pieces on the radiator grille, plated stoneguards on the rear wings and improved bumpers. Various interior and mechanical modifications were also made. Shown are actors Anne Todd and Nigel Patrick beside a Mark V Minx in a scene from the famous David Lean Cineguild film production 'The Sound Barrier'.

31A Hillman Minx

31C Jensen Interceptor

31B Humber Pullman

31B: **Humber** Pullman Mark III (shown) and Imperial Mark III were similar in most respects Wheelbase was 10 ft 11 in, engine a 100-bhp 4-litre OHV Six. Both were eight-seaters, bodied by Thrupp & Maberly. Other contemporary Humbers were the Hawk Mark IV and Super Snipe Mark III.

31C: **Jensen** Interceptor Saloon was a hardtop version of the Interceptor Cabriolet (see 1951) with fabric covered roof and fixed quarter windows. The Saloon had extra leg room because the rear seat was located farther back than on the Cabriolet which had to accommodate the hood (top) recess.

32A Jowett Jupiter

32A/B : Jowett Jupiter. The Jowett company—founded by Benjamin and William Jowett and A. V. Lamb on £30—had completed fifty years. The successful Jupiter was continued with detail modifications including a redesigned fascia/instrument panel. Shown are—32A—an example of a production-bodied Jupiter (photographed at a car rally during the sixties) and—32B—a special-bodied version by J. J. Armstrong of Carlisle. Other specialist coachbuilders also adapted the Jupiter chassis, including Abbott of Farnham, J. E. Farr & Son of Blackburn and Richard Meade of Knowle, Warwicks.

32B Jowett Jupiter

32C Lanchester Leda

32C : Lanchester Leda Series LJ201 Saloon was introduced in April 1952, solely for the export market. Externally identical to the Fourteen (*see* 1951) it differed in having an all-steel body instead of the wood and metal construction of the regular Barker-bodied models. It was discontinued in April 1953.

33C Morris Oxford

33A MG 1¼-Litre YB

33B Morgan Plus Four

33A: **MG** 1¼-Litre Series YB Saloon superseded the 1947–51 Series Y model for 1952. The only major change was the fitting of a hypoid rear axle in place of the spiral bevel type. It was powered by a single-carburettor version of the popular MG 1250-cc OHV engine and featured as standard a sliding roof and an opening windscreen. Discontinued in the summer of 1953.

33B: **Morgan** Plus Four, Four-Seater Tourer was an addition to the existing range (Tourer and Coupé). Generally similar to the two-seater sports models it differed mainly by having two extra seats, with the petrol tank carried beneath, a single spare wheel (two on the Sports) and a single 12-volt battery under the bonnet.

33C: **Morris** Oxford MO Traveller Estate Car made its appearance in September 1952 and is shown with the then current radiator grille. From October all Oxford models had a restyled grille with two horizontal bars (see 1953). The Traveller had the same 1476-cc side-valve engine as the contemporary Oxford Saloon. Other Morris cars at this time were the Minor, which in late 1952 received an OHV engine (Series II), and the 2·2-litre Model MS Six.

34A : **Rolls-Royce** Silver Wraith Touring Limousine. In common with the export-only Silver Dawn and the Mark VI Bentley, this model was fitted with the larger (4566-cc) engine for 1952. Various catalogued bodies were available, including this Touring Limousine by Hooper.

34B : **Rover** 75 Series P4 Saloon. Modifications for the 1952 season included a neater frontal appearance with a new vertical-slat radiator grille—the central fog lamp was deleted—flanked by headlamps mounted in circular instead of square recesses in the wing valances, with the sidelamps located atop the wings. The size of the rear window was increased. The 2103-cc six-cylinder engine had overhead inlet and inclined side exhaust valves and produced 75 bhp at 4200 rpm.

34C : **Singer** SM 1500 Saloon continued virtually unchanged from previous year, during which the interior had received a face-lift and the engine was given a reduction in stroke (89·4 *v.* 90 mm) to bring it under the 1500-cc rating (1497 *v.* 1506 cc). This engine modification also applied to the export-only Roadster (*see* 1953). The SM1500 Saloon was originally introduced in 1948 and continued until 1954. In January 1952 the headlamps were raised.

34D : **Standard** Vanguard (Series 20S) Saloon was given something of an external face-lift for 1952 with the adoption of a slightly lower bonnet line, a wide almost rectangular chrome-plated air-intake with a central horizontal bar, a wider rear window and push button door handles.

34B Rover 75

34C Singer SM 1500

34A Rolls-Royce Silver Wraith

34D Standard Vanguard

35A : **Standard** Vanguard Estate Car for 1952 received the same face-lift as the Saloon (*see* 34D). Known as the Phase I models, this range was superseded by revised Phase II models early in 1953.

35B/C : **Vauxhall** Velox (Model EIP) and Wyvern (Model EIX) Saloons, announced in August 1951, were the first really new post-war Vauxhall models. They featured full-width body styling, curved windscreen, 8 ft 7 in wheelbase and coil spring and wishbone independent front suspension. All doors were hinged at their front edges and had pushbutton catches. The four-cylinder $1\frac{1}{2}$-litre-engined Wyvern was distinguished externally from the six-cylinder $2\frac{1}{4}$-litre-engined Velox by having wheels finished in body colours (cream on Velox) body-coloured flashes on the front wings (chromium on Velox) and different badges. As before the body was of unitary construction but separate chassis were produced for export to Australia where locally-made Tourer bodywork was fitted. The bonnet could be opened from either side or removed altogether (until June 1953 when an alligator-type bonnet was introduced).

35A Standard Vanguard

35B Vauxhall Velox

35C Vauxhall Wyvern

1953

1953 For the first time since the war the British motoring public could go to the Earls Court Motor Show—October 1952—to view the models for the coming year with the feeling that it was once again meant for them as well as their overseas contemporaries. Although, of course, the export markets continued to be uppermost in the minds of manufacturers there was an atmosphere of real optimism that the home-based buyer was at least going to get a look in. The awareness of new competition both at home and abroad was reflected in the number of quite new models available from British manufacturers which included the Allard Palm Beach, Armstrong Siddeley Sapphire, Austin-Healey 100, Bentley Continental, Sunbeam Alpine and Wolseley Four-Forty Four. Some remarkably high speeds were recorded by a number of British models during the year, albeit in modified form, including an Austin-Healey 100 which clocked 142·6 mph and a Jaguar XK120 topping 174 mph! The total number of cars produced in the UK in 1953 was a record 594,808. Of these more than half were exported, namely 307,368. Just over 2000 cars were imported and the total of new car registrations was 306,483 (including 5129 hackneys).

36A: **AC** 2-Litre four-door Saloon was introduced on the British market in October 1952. It was similar to the two-door version (from 1947) but fitted with narrower doors hung from the centre pillar. The 1991-cc triple-carburettor engine developed 76 bhp at 4500 rpm. The two-door model was discontinued in 1956, the four-door in 1958.

36B: **Allard** Palm Beach Tourer, an Open three-seater sports model available with either a Ford Consul 1508-cc Four (Type 21 C) or a Ford Zephyr 2622-cc Six (Type 21 Z) power unit. Fitted with fully-enveloping bodywork, this model was something entirely new for the Allard company which had, since its inception, favoured powerful V8 engines for their high-performance cars.

Wheelbase was 96 in and weight (dry) was 1800 lb (21 C) or 1900 lb (21 Z). 36C: **Allard** K3 Tourer. Fitted with Ford V8 3622-cc 95-bhp power unit as standard, but also available with Lincoln, Cadillac or Chrysler V8 engine at customers' request, this full-width bodied grand tourer was launched—mainly for export—in October 1952, replacing the 1950–52 Model K2. A somewhat later model is shown.

36A AC 2-Litre

36B Allard Palm Beach

36C Allard K3

37A: Armstrong Siddeley Sapphire 346 Saloon. Available with either a four- or six-light body, this luxuriously furnished five/six-seater featured a six-cylinder 3·4-litre 120-bhp engine, a four-speed synchromesh or electrically-operated preselector gearbox, coil spring and wishbone IFS, a built-in heating/demisting and air-conditioning system, fog lamps and a reversing lamp. The two body styles—identical except for the window arrangements—had long sweeping front wings running to meet fully-spatted rear wings, yet retained the traditional radiator grille. The earlier Whitley and Hurricane models were continued.

37A Armstrong Siddeley Sapphire 346

37B Austin A135 Princess

37B: Austin A135 Princess, Model DM4, Limousine. Long-wheelbase model, introduced in October 1952. This Vanden Plas coachbuilt model —an addition to the 3·9-litre engined saloon and touring limousine (from 1948)—had an overall length some 20 in greater than the other two models and had seating for nine. The chassis was used also for special bodywork, e.g. ambulances and hearses.

37C: Austin-Healey 100, Model BN1. Powered by a 2660-cc, 90-bhp four-cylinder engine, this very attractive, sleek two-seater went on show to the general public on the Healey stand at the 1952 Earls Court Motor Show and was designated the Healey Hundred. The demand completely swamped the Donald Healey Motor Company Ltd, to the extent that the Austin Motor Co. offered to take over the manufacture of the car. By the end of the show, the Healey Hundred had become the Austin-Healey 100. Production commenced in 1953 and was continued until mid-1956 when the car was superseded by the 100 Six. From October 1954 a special export model—the 100S—was available, followed in October 1955 by the 100M which featured a LeMans engine modification kit.

37C Austin-Healey 100

38A Bentley Continental

38A : **Bentley** Continental Sports Saloon. Entirely new variant with light-alloy bodywork by H. J. Mulliner. Based on the chassis of the Mark VI Saloon (apart from a higher engine compression ratio and higher final drive ratio) this two-door four-seater had a lower body with long rear wings and sloping 'fastback' rear end styling. It was powered by a modified version of the larger 4566-cc engine, introduced the previous year, which greatly improved the performance and power output. The traditional dummy filler cap and winged 'B' mascot were eliminated from the radiator shell.

38B : **Bentley** R Type Saloon. Also known as the B7, this four-door model differed from the Mark VI Saloon mainly in having a lengthened and more elegant tail with the spare wheel housed in a tray under the larger boot.

38B Bentley R Type

38C/D : **Bristol** 403 Saloon, introduced in May 1953, was identical in appearance to the 401 (*see* 1950), except for a silver grille, red medallions and the 403 scipt on the sides of the bodywork. In addition, the 1971-cc engine produced more power (100 bhp at 5400 rpm), the braking was improved and a front anti-roll bar was fitted. The Bristol 401/403 is regarded by many as one of the most beautiful British cars ever made.

38C Bristol 403

38D Bristol 403

39A Citroën Big Fifteen

39C Ford Prefect

39A : **Citroën** Big Fifteen Saloon. One of the popular front-wheel-drive cars of French origin, assembled in England at Slough, Bucks. Development of a pre-war favourite, this version was re-introduced in October 1952 (it had originally been re-introduced in France in 1947). Fitted with the same engine as the Light Fifteen Saloon (*see* 6E)—1911-cc, developing 55·7 bhp at 4250 rpm—the Big Fifteen had the same wheelbase and main body shell of the six-cylinder 2·8-litre model (1948—55).

39B : **Daimler** Conquest Series DJ Saloon. Replacement for the Consort, this six-seater model used main body pressings identical to those of the Lanchester 14 (*see* 21B). The new 2·4-litre engine which produced 75 bhp at 4000 rpm gave the Conquest sporting performance and handling, although from the point of view of styling and finish it was very much in the Daimler tradition.

39C : **Ford** Prefect Model E493A (shown) and the smaller two-door Anglia Model E494 were in their last year of production; they were superseded by the New Prefect and New Anglia 100E in October. An economy version of the Anglia, with the old type Prefect engine, was however kept in production, designated Popular 103E.

39D : **Frazer-Nash** Targa Florio Turismo was a high-speed touring car with entirely new full-width body styling. The windscreen, although not shown, was similar to that of the Mille Miglia model. Named after the famous race because a Frazer-Nash, in 1951, became the first British car to win this event. Also available to full competition specification—Gran Sport—including bucket seats and more powerful engine.

39B Daimler Conquest

39D Frazer-Nash Targa Florio Turismo

40A: **Hillman** Minx Mark VI Convertible Coupé (shown) and Saloon were the Minx's 21st anniversary models, featuring new frontal treatment (higher, oval, curved radiator grille), round rear lamps that faired into the wings and a redesigned fascia with a chromium surround. An Estate Car version was also available.

40B: **Hillman** Minx Californian Hardtop was a new model, similar to the Convertible Coupé but fitted with a fixed metal roof and a large wrap-round three-piece rear window. The side windows wound down into the body panels, with no centre body pillar. It followed a style that had been popularized in the USA.

40C Hillman Special

40A Hillman Minx

40C: **Hillman** with a difference. This Special was designed and built in the workshop of H. E. Robinson & Co., Ltd of Trinidad, by their service manager S. G. Thompson. Built almost entirely of Minx parts it had a claimed top speed of 106 mph !

40D: **Humber** Super Snipe Mark IV Saloon for 1953 featured a completely redesigned body of the full-width type, a new chassis with coil spring and wishbone IFS, and an entirely new 4-litre, six-cylinder OHV engine which developed 113 bhp at the unusually low speed of 3400 rpm. Shown is HRH The late Duke of Windsor's special Super Snipe leaving the works of Thrupp & Maberly Ltd (coachbuilders) before departing for Paris—May 1953.

40B Hillman Minx Californian

40D Humber Super Snipe

41A Jaguar XK120

41B Jowett Javelin

41A: **Jaguar** XK120 Drophead Coupé. Differed from the Sports two-seater mainly in having more fittings, wind-up windows and a fully-folding and properly trimmed top. It was also some $2\frac{1}{4}$ cwt heavier. In production between March 1953 and October 1954.

41B: **Jowett** Javelin PE Saloon replaced the PD model from October 1952 and was powered by the Series III flat-4 1486-cc engine, which was a great improvement over the troublesome earlier versions. Sturdier tapered-section bumpers were fitted and leather upholstery became standard on the basic as well as the de Luxe model. It was in this form that the Javelin—and indeed Jowett—production run ended in 1953/54. Shown is a beautifully kept example on display at a 1973 Sussex car rally.

41C: **Jowett** Jupiter Mark IA (Series SC). Also fitted with a Series III power unit this model, which replaced the Mark I (Series SA) in October 1952, featured numerous modifications including a proper opening boot, smoother wings, larger cockpit, curved mouldings only over the front wheel arches and metal fascia panel with grouped instruments.

41C Jowett Jupiter

42A Lagonda 2½-Litre

42B Lanchester Fourteen

42C Lanchester Dauphin

42A: **Lagonda** 2½-Litre Saloon and Drophead Coupé (shown) were six-cylinder-engined luxury cars with all-independent suspension, first announced in 1946. Although retaining the general lines of previous models, the Mark II Saloon (from Oct. 1952) had a smoother and altogether tidier appearance and featured a number of notable improvements including repositioning of components beneath the bonnet to improve accessibility, revised instrument panel, wider rear seat, improved heating and demisting equipment and hydraulic jacks. The Saloon was discontinued in June 1953, the Mark I Coupé (bodied by Tickford) two months later. During the year a few Coupés were produced to Mark II specification.

42B: **Lanchester** Fourteen Drophead Coupé was based on the Saloon (*see* 21B). This two-door 'De Ville Convertible' model, featured a part-power-operated top as standard and had a dry weight some 84 lb higher than the saloon. Both models were discontinued in the summer of 1954.

42C: **Lanchester** Dauphin prototype Saloon, Model LJ250, was a two-door Hooper-bodied model with 2433-cc twin-carb engine and light alloy bodywork. It was not made in quantity.

43A Morris Minor

43B Morris Oxford

43A: **Morris** Minor Series II was available as two- or four-door Saloon and two-door Convertible. The arrival of the series II—unchanged externally from the preceding Series MM—heralded the switch from the old 918·6-cc side-valve engine to the smaller yet more powerful 803-cc OHV unit (similar to the Austin A30 engine but with an SU carburettor)—made possible following the merger between Nuffield and Austin (BMC) in the latter half of 1951. In October 1953 the Traveller Estate Car made its debut.

43B: **Morris** Oxford Series MO was available in Saloon (shown) and Estate Car (Traveller) variants. The latter had an ash-framed light alloy panelled body with sliding rear windows and vertically-hinged double back doors (*see* 33C). Both the estate and saloon were fitted with a new chromium-plated radiator grille of different design to the zinc-alloy type used on previous Oxfords.

43C: **Rolls-Royce** Silver Dawn 4½-Litre Saloon. First introduced in 1949—with the 4¼-litre engine—to meet the export demand for a 'smaller' version of the Wraith, it did not in fact become available on the home market until the autumn of 1953 by which time it had acquired the 4½-litre engine and the longer body of the R Type Bentley.

43C Rolls-Royce Silver Dawn

44A Singer SM1500

44B Singer SMX

44A: Singer SM1500 Roadster, Model 4AD, looked identical to the Singer Nine Roadster, but had a 1497-cc power unit and detail differences. First introduced as an export-only model early in 1951, it did not become available on the home market until January 1953. During 1952 the width of the radiator grille slats was reduced and the pressure of the cooling system raised to correct earlier overheating problems.

44B: Singer SMX Roadster was an experimental plastic-bodied sports model, shown at the 1953 London Motor Show. Fitted with a twin-carburettor version of the 1½-litre engine, it was longer and lighter than the SM1500 Roadster which it was to replace. It did not get beyond the prototype stage, however, and this was the only one ever built.

44C: Standard Vanguard Phase II Saloon, Series 20S. This extensively modified version was announced in January 1953. External changes included complete restyling of the back of the car, deletion of the lower of the three radiator grille cross bars, extension of the grille to take in the side lights, and the fitting of a bullet-shaped bonnet ornament. Mechanical modifications were made to engine, clutch, steering and suspension. The Phase II Estate Car variant appeared in February.

44C Standard Vanguard

45A Sunbeam Alpine

45A/B : **Sunbeam** Alpine Mark IIA Sports Roadster was named after the tough international rally in which the Sunbeam-Talbot 90 had been so successful. Introduced in March 1953, the Alpine was initially available only for export, most of them going to America. It was based on the 90 mechanically but with differences such as a tuned version of the 2267-cc engine, strengthened chassis and suspension, modified gearbox ratios and a straight-through silencer. The entirely new two-seater body was similar in general outline to the 90 Convertible but was immediately distinguishable by its louvred bonnet top and long rear decking. Either a single-pane windscreen plus side panels, or a curved transparent-plastic racing screen could be fitted ; both are shown.

45C : **Sunbeam-Talbot** 90 Mark IIA Saloon. Modifications introduced on this version—announced in September 1952—included perforated disc wheels with new chrome hub caps and rim embellishers, the deletion of the rear-wheel spats and the fitting of larger brakes. The Convertible version was similarly modified.

45B Sunbeam Alpine

45C Sunbeam-Talbot 90

46A: **Triumph** Sports (prototype, Model 20SR). Forerunner of the Triumph TR2 (*see* pages 62 and 63) this 2-litre-engined sports car was first shown at the 1952 London Motor Show. The two-seater bodywork featured a rectangular open air-intake at the front, long front wings and a short rounded tail on which the spare wheel was mounted; it was supported by the fuel tank filler pipe. Luggage space was very limited. Only two were built.

46A Triumph Sports (prototype)

46B Triumph 2000 Renown

46C Wolseley Four-Forty Four

46B: **Triumph** 2000 Renown Saloon, Model 20ST, had superseded the similar-looking 1800 Saloon (18T) in 1949 and was continued in production until 1954/55. It had attractive knife-edge body styling and during Oct. 1951—Oct. 1952 a Limousine version had been available. The latter had 3-in longer wheelbase (9 ft 3 in) and from early 1952 this size was adopted also for the Saloon (20STA).

46C: **Wolseley** Four-Forty Four Saloon was a replacement for the Four-Fifty (1948—53) and featured a 1250-cc OHV engine which developed 46 bhp at 4800 rpm, unitary construction, coil-spring IFS, and dimensions that made it longer, narrower and lower than its predecessor, although the wheelbase was the same.

47A AC Ace

47A : **AC** Ace, announced in October 1953, was a two-seater based on the successful sports and racing cars of designer/builder John Tojeiro. Powered by a tuned version of the 2-litre six-cylinder AC engine it was the first post-war British sports car with all-independent suspension (transverse leaf springs, front and rear). The attractive all-enveloping bodywork was of light-alloy mounted on a tubular steel frame. The fully-carpeted cockpit was well equipped and the hood (top) canvas and its separate frame could be stowed in the tail of the body when not in use. Centre-lock wire wheels were fitted as standard. By the time it went into full production in 1954 certain modifications had been incorporated, including high-mounted headlamps, a recessed raked-back grille and a stronger frame.

47B : **Allard** Coachbuilt Saloon, a one-off two-door streamlined aluminium-panelled model built by E. D. Abbott of Farnham on the Palm Beach chassis. It featured a curved windscreen, and headlamps and sidelamps mounted within a wide front air-intake.

1954 It was significant that of the record total British car output for the year little over 52% was allocated for the export market compared with the 75%–80% of the more critical post-war years. The unexpected rise in domestic car buying, unfortunately, merely accelerated another pressing problem—serious congestion on the already inadequate British roads.

The number of new models introduced during the year continued to rise—a sure sign that the Government-encouraged policy of 'one model one make' during the post-war years had been forgotten —as indeed it had to be if the country were to compete successfully in the increasingly competitive world markets. Ford reclaimed their 'cheapest car' title with the announcement of the Popular which sold at just £390 14s 2d—about 20% lower than its nearest competitor. Notable additions to the British model line-up included the AC Ace, Bristol 404, Jensen 541, MG ZA Magnette, Riley Pathfinder and Triumph TR2.

During the Calendar year the British Motor Industry turned out a total of 769,165 cars and 268,714 commercial vehicles. Export figures totalled 372,029 and 118,796 respectively (plus 145 and 1417 used units resp.).

Imports rose to 4660 cars and 684 commercial vehicles (1953: 2067 and 49 resp.). New car registrations in 1954 amounted to 394,362, plus 5593 hackneys.

47B Allard Coachbuilt Saloon

48A: **Alvis** TC 21/100 Grey Lady Saloon, a new
model based on the standard Three Litre TC 21 ;
differences included an increase in engine compression
ratio (8·0:1 v. 7·0:1) and max. bhp (100 v. 93), higher
rear axle ratio, bonnet-top scoops, bonnet-side louvres
and wire wheels with knock-off hubs to give extra
cooling for the brake drums. A Tickford-bodied
Drophead Coupé was also available. The TC 21 was
continued with restyled body features which it shared
with the Grey Lady until October 1954, when it was
discontinued.

48B Aston Martin DB2-4

48B: **Aston Martin** DB2-4
Saloon (shown) and Drophead
Coupé were fitted with the 125-
bhp Vantage engine as standard
(it had been optional on the
superseded DB2). Although the
main mechanical features and the
front and centre section of the
chassis were basically the same as
on the DB2, the rear of the car
was completely redesigned. In
addition to having two additional
(emergency) seats it had a large
luggage platform accessible via a
tailgate which was hinged above a
greatly enlarged rear window.
Later production models had a 3-litre
(2922-cc) engine as standard.
Wheelbase was 8 ft 3 in.

48A Alvis TC21/100 Grey Lady

49A : **Austin** A30 Model AS4 two-door Saloon joined the four-door Saloon in October 1953. Both models had a completely restyled interior (including redesigned fascia and parcel shelf, increased knee and headroom, wider front seats and improved trim) and an increase in luggage boot capacity.

49B : **Austin** Champ Model WN1 $\frac{1}{4}$-ton 4 × 4 field car was produced in large numbers for the British Army and powered by a standardized Rolls-Royce B40 four-cylinder engine. During 1952–56 Austin also offered a civilian version (Model WN3), with their own A90 engine, civilian-style instrument panel and non-folding windscreen. Shown is one of the many military models which later found their way to Civvy Street.

49B Austin Champ

49A Austin A30

49C Bentley R Type

49C : **Bentley** R Type Sports Saloon. Version shown featured coachwork by E. D. Abbott of Farnham, in panelled aluminium over a strong ash frame mounted on a steel sub-frame. Unladen weight was approx. 36 cwt.

50: **Bristol** 404 Fixed Head Coupé model joined the 403 Saloon in the autumn of 1953. It was a handsome short-wheelbase two/four-seater (occasional small rear seats could be folded down to take extra luggage), powered by the 1971-cc engine with 8·5:1 compression ratio as standard and featuring a light-alloy panelled body on a wooden frame (the doors had aluminium frames). The tail-fin-like extensions on the rear wings were functional (for aerodynamic stability) and not merely decorative. The Bristol 403 and 404 were discontinued in October 1955.

51A Citroën 2CV

51A: Citroën 2CV was first introduced in France in 1949 and became available in the UK—Slough-built version—in October 1953. Described by some people as a latter-day equivalent of the Model T Ford, this novel and economical little car had an air-cooled flat-twin four-stroke 375-cc (later 425-cc) engine, driving the front wheels, all-independent yet interlinked suspension, a 'push and twist' gearchange and a four-speed gearbox with overdrive top. The body was of very light construction, with a fabric roof, four doors and four seats.

51B: Daimler Conquest Series DJ Roadster and Drophead Coupé (shown) were introduced in October 1953 respectively. Both models were mechanically based on the Conquest Saloon (see 39B), but incorporated certain differences including a twin-carburettor high-compression 100-bhp version of the 2·4-litre power unit, larger brakes and a large diameter propeller shaft. The lightweight body construction was achieved by the use of aluminium-alloy framework, aluminium panelling and wings.

51C: Daimler Conquest Century Series DJ Saloon was a high-performance version of the Conquest Saloon, mechanically similar to the Roadster and Coupé (51B) and distinguishable from the Conquest mainly by chromium-plated windscreen and rear-window frames, and deeper bumpers. All models featured Daimler's pre-selector fluid transmission, the control lever of which was mounted on the steering column, as shown.

51B Daimler Conquest

51C Daimler Conquest Century

52A Ford Prefect

52B Ford Anglia

52A : **Ford** Prefect Model 100E four-door Saloon. Introduced in October 1953 and powered by a new side-valve 1172-cc 36-bhp engine it had low full-width body styling with a vertically-slatted chrome grille. The front wings and the lower part of each rear wing were separate parts bolted to the main body shell—a useful asset in accident repair work. The new independent front suspension was evolved from that of the Consul and Zephyr; conventional leaf springs were fitted at the rear.

52B : **Ford** Anglia 100E Saloon. Announced simultaneously with the Prefect (52A), this two-door version was mechanically identical and used the same basic body shell. At the front it was distinguishable by the radiator grille which comprised three horizontal silver-painted bars. Less comprehensively equipped than the four-door Prefect it weighed about ½ cwt less. Also available was the Popular which had a similar body to the old Anglia but was powered by the old Prefect engine (previously used for export Anglias).

52C : **Ford** Zephyr Six models for 1954 had a wing-type bonnet ornament, a flat front bumper centre section, flasher-type direction indicators and a few other changes.

52C Ford Zephyr Six

53 : **Ford** Zodiac Model EOTTA Saloon was a high-performance luxury edition of the Zephyr Six Saloon, added to the range in October 1953. Officially billed as the Zephyr-Zodiac it featured a 71-bhp engine with 7·5 :1 compression ratio and was externally distinguishable by a two-tone colour scheme and white-wall tyres. Standard equipment included leather upholstery, fog and spot lamps, cigar lighter and clock.

53 Ford Zodiac

54A Frazer-Nash Sebring

54A : **Frazer-Nash** Sebring Sports. Developed from the Mark II Competition model, this model was powered by the 2-litre Bristol engine and had a light alloy all-enveloping body. It took its name from the 12-hour endurance race at Sebring, USA, which had been won by Frazer-Nash in 1952. At the wheel in the version shown is W. H. Aldington who, together with his brother, took over control of production of the chain-drive Frazer-Nash in the late 'twenties'.

54B : **Hillman** Minx Mark VII Saloon superseded the Mark VI and differed mainly in appearance; the rear wings were longer and carried more angular rear lamp clusters, the rear window was larger and the luggage capacity was increased as a result of the reshaped boot. The two-door Drophead Coupé version was similarly modified.

54C : **Hillman** Minx Mark VII Californian Hardtop. This attractive model featured modifications similar to those of the Minx Saloon (*q.v.*). From October all Minx models, except the Special and Estate Car, were fitted with a 1390-cc OHV engine and redesignated Mark VIII.

54B Hillman Minx

54C Hillman Minx Californian

55A Humber Hawk

55B Humber Super Snipe

55A: **Humber** Hawk Mark VI Saloon.
Introduced in June 1954 this model had an
OHV version of the 2267-cc engine with a
7·0:1 compression ratio, which increased its
output to 70 bhp (preceding side-valve version
produced 58 bhp). Other modifications included
bigger brakes, better interior trim, raised rear
wing line, larger rear lamp units and a chrome
strip along the front wings. Shown is a brace of
Hawks with owners Signor Bruscantini (left)
and Mr Ian Wallace—stars of the Glyndebourne
Opera Co.—in Edinburgh in 1954.

55B: **Humber** Super Snipe Mark IV. Super
Snipe models were continued with only minor
changes. Shown is an impressive custom-built
estate car based on this chassis. The Super
Snipe was discontinued in 1956 but was
revived again in the late 1950s.

55C: **Jaguar** D-type (Series XKD) Sports/
Roadster. This famous competition model came
off the secret list in the spring of 1954, to
replace the highly successful XK120C (*see*
20C). The 3442-cc triple-carburettor power unit
developed 250 bhp (some models had fuel
injection). Shown are three of the 1954 Le
Mans D-type entries ready to do battle on the
track—No. 14 (Holt/Hamilton) came second
behind a Ferrari. The D-type did not become
available until the autumn of 1954—and then
only to selected customers.

55C Jaguar D-type

56A Jensen 541

56A : **Jensen** 541, an entirely new car with 4-litre engine which joined the Interceptor—continued with minor improvements—in the autumn of 1953. Apart from the engine/gearbox unit, the 541 was an entirely new design. The more compact arrangement of the chassis gave it a shorter wheelbase and reduced track. This distinctive 'close coupled saloon' featured a sleek, long, rounded body with a wide wrap-round window at the rear which gave exceptional visibility for the driver. The wide oval grille was fitted with a pivoted blanking-plate which was merely a radiator shutter, albeit a more attractive and effective one. The 541 did not in fact go into production until late 1954/early 1955, by which time its steel body had been dropped in favour of a glass-fibre-reinforced plastic version.

56B Jowett Jupiter

56B : **Jowett** Jupiter R4 was revealed at the 1953 Earls Court show, by which time Javelin production had ceased owing to difficulties with the supply of body shells. Although the overall design was totally different from the Type IA (*see* 41C), the power units used were very similar. The car had a broad squat two-seater body shell, with a wide oval grille, fitted to a deep box-section chassis frame. Only three cars were ever made. The R4 was the last car to bear the Jowett name, for production finally came to a halt in 1954.

56C Lagonda Three Litre

56C : **Lagonda** Three Litre, Series I, was announced in October 1953, following the enthusiasm for the 2½-litre Tickford-bodied Coupé of the previous year. Longer and lower than the 2½-Litre model which it replaced, the Three Litre had a full-width body with the traditional Lagonda grille. Available initially in two-door Saloon and Drophead Coupé form—a four-door Tickford Saloon was introduced in October 1954. Production of the two-door Saloon ceased in late 1954 (Drophead Coupé in 1956). During 1956–58 a Series II four-door Saloon was made.

57A: **Lanchester** Sprite I Saloon, a prototype model—three were built—fitted with a 1·6-litre four-cylinder version of the Daimler Conquest engine coupled with a Hobbs automatic transmission. Although the first British light car ever to have a fully automatic transmission system, it was given a cool reception generally and did not go into production. Ironically, only ten of the Mark II version, which replaced it in 1955, were produced because Lanchester ceased operating later that year.

57A Lanchester Sprite

57B/C: **Land-Rover**
Series I 86 Station Wagon was introduced in April 1954 (there had been a Station Wagon available on the earlier 80-in wheelbase chassis during 1948–51). The new wagon was a modification of the contemporary short-wheelbase (86-in) Land-Rover Regular 4 × 4 multi-purpose vehicle, which had a 1997-cc four-cylinder petrol engine. In August this engine was brought in line with that of the Rover 60 car (spread-bore cylinder block).

57B Land-Rover 86

57C Land-Rover 86

57D: **MG** Magnette ZA superseded the Series Y saloon in October 1953. Powered by a 1½-litre 60-bhp BMC B-Series engine it had outward similarities to its BMC relative, the Wolseley 4/44 (*see* 46C), though it was lower and had a curved facsimile of the traditional MG radiator. It weathered initial criticism from MG purists and went on to become a very popular and sought-after-car. In late 1956 it was superseded in production by the slightly modified ZB standard and Varitone saloons. The latter had two-tone paintwork and a wrap-round rear window.

57D MG Magnette

58A MG Midget TF

58: MG Midget TF two-seater Sports. Replacement for the TD its detail changes including an improved, lower bonnet line that sloped down to a tidier, raked-back radiator; the headlamps were faired into the front wing valances. Other improvements included a better top, individually adjustable seats and increased engine power.

58B Morgan Plus Four

58B: Morgan Plus Four continued with modified front end treatment— partly cowled and curved grille and with the headlamps faired into the wing valances. Also available in 1954, for the two-seater Sports only, was the TR2 (1991-cc) engine; this power unit did not become available on the Drophead Coupé and four-seater Tourer models until late 1955.

58C: Morris Minor Series II Traveller. New variant with shooting-brake style body-work. The ash body frame was panelled in aluminium— from the driving compart-ment back. The rear seat

58C Morris Minor

folded flat to give additional luggage space. The wheelbase size was the same as the other Morris Minor models, namely 7 ft 2 in.

58D Morris Oxford

58D: Morris Oxford Series II Saloon. Powered by the BMC B-Series 1½-litre 50-bhp OHV engine it had a new mono-construction body which, although having the same wheelbase and track as the preceding Series MO, was much roomier. The Morris Six was discontinued in March 1954—some two months before the announcement of the Series II Oxford. In July 1954 a simplified version of the Oxford appeared, named the Cowley; this model had the 1200-cc engine which also powered the contemporary Austin A40 range of models.

59 Riley Pathfinder

59: **Riley** Pathfinder Model RMH four-door Saloon was introduced in October 1953 and produced until early 1957. It superseded the 1946–53 2½-Litre model; the 1½-Litre Saloon was continued with restyled front wings, rear wing spats, elimination of running boards, etc. The Pathfinder had entirely new full-width bodywork (used also on the Wolseley Six-Ninety from October 1954) on a new chassis with torsion bar IFS and coil spring rear suspension. The engine was an improved development from the earlier 100-bhp 2½-litre unit, now developing 110 bhp.

60A : **Rolls-Royce** Silver Dawn Drophead Coupé, by H. J. Mulliner. In October 1953 the Silver Dawn model became available on the home market, more than four years after its original announcement; all those built previously had been for export only. It was discontinued in the spring of 1955, in favour of the new Silver Cloud model.

60B : **Rover** 90, Series P4. In August 1953, Rover launched the 90 (shown) and 60 Saloons as alternative-engined versions of the existing 75 model, the bodywork and chassis being common to all three. The 90 model was powered by a 2638-cc 90-bhp engine and the 60 by a 1997-cc 60-bhp unit; all had four cylinders. Modifications made to the 75—also incorporated on the other two versions—included a central lever gearchange, repositioned handbrake, and synchromesh on second gear as well as third and top. The 90 could be distinguished externally by the badge on the scuttle and the long-range lamp on the front bumper. Wheelbase was 9 ft 3 in, tyre size 6·00-15. NOTE: for Land-Rover *see* page 57.

Rolls-Royce "Silver Dawn" Drop-head Coupé

60A Rolls-Royce Silver Dawn

60B Rover 90

61A: **Standard** Eight Saloon was vastly different from its earlier namesake (1945–48). This later version marked Standard's return to the small-car market after an absence of five years. The new car was powered by an 803-cc OHV engine and fitted with a full-width body of somewhat snub appearance. Very much an economy car it was sold, initially, minus wheel hub covers, nearside sun visor and windscreen wiper, tool roll and all but basic interior trim and equipment. A less austere version was, however, added in the spring of 1954 and a Standard Ten Saloon—with 948 cc engine—joined the Eight at the same time.

61B/C: **Sunbeam-Talbot** 90 Mark IIA Saloon and Drophead Coupé continued with detail changes including the Alpine's higher compression ratio, modified front bumper, and plated surrounds on the small side grilles on the front valance. From October 1954 both models carried the marque name Sunbeam (Mark III), thus falling into line with the Alpine Roadster which had been designated Sunbeam from its introduction in early 1953. (*See* page 45.)

61B Sunbeam-Talbot 90

61A Standard Eight

61C Sunbeam-Talbot 90

1954

Power graced by elegance

SPEED Packed into the 2 litre engine of the Swallow Doretti is all the surging power needed to send the miles scudding behind. Although capable of over 100 miles an hour the car is ideal for fast touring at 75 to 90 m.p.h., at the same time high performance is combined with exceptionally economical running.

COMFORT Controls and steering are so arranged to give maximum comfort for the driver, while the interior is luxuriously fitted with leather covered sponge rubber moulding, first quality hide upholstery and thick carpeting.

SAFETY The 50-ton tubular steel chassis of the Swallow Doretti is specially built to meet the stresses of high-speed motoring and to ensure the greatest possible stability; hydraulic brakes are also fitted, thus you can drive this fine car knowing that every device to provide the greatest possible safety has been incorporated.

STYLE Friends will stop and admire the smooth, sleek lines of your Swallow Doretti. Beautifully styled on the classical Sports Car lines it provides the utmost in elegance.

Swallow Doretti

The sports car you will be proud to own

Price £777.0s.0d.   P.T. £324.17s.6d.
For name of nearest Distributor write or phone to:
THE SWALLOW COACHBUILDING COMPANY (1935) LTD.
The Airport, Walsall, Staffs. Walsall 4553

ABOVE is shown the luxurious interior of the Swallow Doretti with controls neatly grouped in front of the driver, while LEFT shows the 50 ton tubular steel chassis that ensures complete stability.

62A Swallow Doretti

62A : Swallow Doretti two-seater Sports was introduced by the Swallow Coachbuilding Co. (1935) Ltd of Walsall, Staffs, in March 1954. Based on mechanical components of the Triumph TR2, the car featured double-skinned bodywork—steel inner shell and aluminium outer shell—with sleek lines and a well-equipped cockpit. A prototype coupé version was also built, but production was discontinued after only one year.

62B : Triumph TR2 power unit was derived from that of the Standard Vanguard. With twin SU carburettors and 8·5 :1 compression ratio, the 1991-cc OHV Four developed 90 bhp at 4800 rpm. It drove the hypoid bevel rear axle through a four-speed gearbox. In 1955 a Laycock-de-Normanville overdrive (on top gear) became available as an optional extra.

62B Triumph TR2

63 : Triumph TR2 Sports, Model 20TR2, was introduced in the summer of 1953—the result of exhaustive test work on the two Triumph Roadster prototypes (*see* 46A). The production model featured a longer, squared-off tail, housing a good-sized luggage boot, and modifications to brakes and chassis frame. The sidelamps were moved to below the headlamps, and the rear lamps raised to the tips of the finned wings. The car quickly established itself in competition work by taking 1st, 2nd and 5th places in the 1954 RAC Rally. A specially tuned TR2 achieved 125 mph on the Jabbeke highway in Belgium.

63 Triumph TR2

INDEX

SUMMARY OF MAJOR BRITISH CAR MAKES
1950–1954 (with dates of their existence)

AC	(from 1908)
Alvis	(1920–67)
Armstrong Siddeley	(1919–60)
Aston Martin	(from 1922)
Austin	(from 1906)
Bentley	(from 1920)
Bristol	(from 1947)
Daimler	(from 1896)
Ford	(from 1911)
Hillman	(from 1907)
Humber	(from 1898)
Jaguar	(from 1932)
Jowett	(1906–54)
Lagonda	(1906–63)
Lanchester	(1895–1956)
Lea-Francis	(1904–60)*
MG	(from 1924)
Morgan	(from 1910)
Morris	(from 1913)
Riley	(1898–1969)
Rolls-Royce	(from 1904)
Rover	(from 1904)
Singer	(1905–70)
Standard	(1903–63)
Sunbeam-Talbot	(1938–54)
Triumph	(from 1923)
Vauxhall	(from 1903)
Wolseley	(from 1911)

*irregularly

ABBREVIATIONS

bhp	brake horsepower
HP	horsepower (RAC rating)
IFS	independent front suspension
OHC	overhead camshaft (engine)
OHV	overhead valves (engine)
q.v.	*quod vide* (which see)

ACKNOWLEDGEMENTS

This book was compiled and written largely from historic source material in the library of the Olyslager Organisation, and in addition photographs were kindly provided by several manufacturers and organisations, notably: AFN Ltd (Mr W. H. Aldington), Allard Owners Club Ltd (Mr David Kinsella), British Leyland UK Ltd (Austin-Morris and Jaguar Divisions), Chiltern Cars, Chrysler UK Ltd, Ford Motor Company Ltd, and Vauxhall Motors Ltd.